Apples

Victoria Blakemore

vblakemore.author@gmail.com

Copyright info/picture credits

Cover, sarsmis/AdobeStock; Page 3, Sasha/AdobeStock; Page 5, Daria-Yakoleva/Pixabay; Page 7, congerdesign/Pixabay; Page 9, Pexels/Pixabay; Page 11, congerdesign/Pixabay; Page 13, Pexels/Pixabay; Page 15, barnafe/Pixabay; Page 17, varintorn/Pixabay; Page 19, alekosa/AdobeStock; Page 21, debramillet/AdobeStock; Page 23; ponce_photography/Pixabay; Page 25, hansenn/AdobeStock; Page 27, Iriana Shiyan/AdobeStock; Page 29, Pixavril/AdobeStock; Page 31, sarsmis/AdobeStock; Page 33, BrentHofacker/AdobeStock

Table of Contents

What are Apples? 2

History of Apples 4

Apple Stems 6

Apple Skin 8

Apple Flesh 10

Apple Seeds 12

Apple Trees 14

Life Cycle 16

Where Are Apples Grown? 18

Growing Apples 20

Transportation 24

Storage 26

Nutrition 28

Health Benefits 30

Eating Apples 32

Glossary 34

What Are Apples?

Apples are fruits that are members of the rose family. Other members of the rose family include cherries, plums, and pears.

There are over 7,500 different kinds of apples. They can be sweet or sour.

Apples can be all different

shades of red, yellow, and green.

History of Apples

Apples are believed to have come from Eastern Europe or Asia. They were brought to America by the Pilgrims.

John Chapman, who is sometimes called "Johnny Appleseed," planted many apple seeds in North America.

Apples are now one of the

most **produced** fruits in the

world.

Apple Stems

The apple stem is the piece

of wood that attaches the

apple to the tree.

Nutrients are transported

through the stem to the

apple as it grows.

Apples that are **ripe** should easily twist off the stem. If they do not, they may not be ripe yet.

Apple Skin

Apple skin is the outside layer of the apple. It can be many shades of red, yellow, and green.

Apples may have dark spots on the skin. These are called **bruises**. They happen when oxygen gets through the skin to the fruit.

Apple Flesh

Apple flesh is the part of the apple that we eat. It is under the skin and is sometimes called the meat of the apple.

When apples are ripe, their flesh is crisp and juicy. Much of the apple flesh is made up of air. This is why apples float in water.

The apple flesh can be sliced

and dried to make apple chips.

Apple Seeds

Apple seeds are small and black. When planted in soil, they may grow into an apple tree.

Apple seeds should never be eaten. They contain a chemical that is **poisonous** to humans and many animals.

The apple seeds are in the

center of the apple. This part

is called the core.

Apple Trees

Fully grown apple trees can be between ten and thirty feet tall.

Dwarf apple trees are smaller than regular apple trees. Many growers prefer them because they grow apples sooner.

Apple trees have flowers that
are called apple blossoms. They
are usually pink and white.

Life Cycle

First, an apple seed is planted in soil. The seed grows into a tree. After about five years, the tree will be fully grown.

Then, it will begin to grow flowers. If they are **pollinated** by bees, part of the flower will grow into an apple.

The apples contain the

seeds that can be used to

plant a new tree.

Where Are Apples Grown?

Apples are grown all over the world. China grows more apples than any country, followed by the United States.

In the United States, the state of Washington grows the most apples.

Apples are grown in over 7,000

orchards in the United States.

They are grown in every state.

Growing Apples

Apples are grown in orchards.
An orchard is land where fruit
or nut trees are grown.

In many orchards, apples are
not grown from seeds. They
are grown from **grafts**, or
parts of another apple tree.

Trees in apple orchards are

often grown in rows.

Apple trees grow best in places with cool temperatures in the winter. They need the cool weather to make sure their blooms open in the spring.

Apple trees bloom in the spring and are ready to be harvested in the fall.

Apples are picked by hand.

They must be handled carefully

so that they don't bruise.

Transportation

When apples are first picked, they are carefully placed in large bins. Apple bins are often kept in the shade to keep the apples cool.

The bins will be transported to places where the apples are sorted and stored.

Bins of apples are often transported from orchards by tractors or trucks.

Storage

Once the apples are brought to the storage building, they need to be sorted. They are checked for bruises, scrapes, and firmness.

The apples are moved through the sorting machines with water so they don't bruise.

Apples are gently loaded back

into bins to be brought to

markets.

Nutrition

Apples are very good for you. They provide your body with **nutrients** such as fiber, vitamin C, vitamin A, vitamin B, and calcium.

They are low in calories and fat, so they are a healthy choice for a snack.

Most of the nutrients are in

the skin, so it is better not to

peel them before eating.

Health Benefits

Apples can help your body to have strong bones and teeth. They can also reduce the risk of heart disease.

The fiber in apples can help your body to get rid of waste.

Eating Apples

Apples can be used to make many different foods. They can make apple juice, cider, baby food, apple butter, and applesauce.

Apples can also be baked into desserts like tarts, cakes, and pies.

Many people bake apple pie

using fresh apples.

Glossary

Bruise: a dark spot on fruit that may be softer than the rest of the fruit

Graft: part of a plant that is cut off and used to grow a new plant

Nutrients: something in food that helps people, animals, and plants grow

Poisonous: likely to cause harm or make someone sick

Pollinated: when pollen is moved from one plant to another, allowing crops to grow

Produced: made, grown

Ripe: ready to be eaten

About the Author

Victoria Blakemore is a first grade

teacher in Southwest Florida with a

passion for reading.

You can visit her at

www.elementaryexplorers.com

Also in This Series

Gray Wolves	Sloths	Flamingos	Camels	Koalas	Honey Bees	Pandas
Pangolins	White-Tailed Deer	Orcas	Giraffes	Corn	Meerkats	Echidnas
Walruses	Raccoons	Bald Eagles	Apples	Arctic Foxes	Red Pandas	Cassowaries
Tigers	Ladybugs	Moose	Beluga Whales	Leopards	Elephants	Jellyfish
Binturongs	Lions	Dolphins	Reindeer	Hammerhead Sharks	Hippos	Pumpkins
Peafowl	Chameleons	Florida Panthers	Aye-Ayes	Black Bears	Cheetahs	Manatees
Gingerbread	Polar Bears	Hot Chocolate	Orangutans	Coyotes	Marshmallows	Strawberries

Victoria Blakemore

Also in This Series

Aardvarks	Mako Sharks	Alligators	Frogs	Hedgehogs	Brown Bears	Bongos
Sea Turtles	Quokkas	Muskrats	Zebras	Red Foxes	Ring-Tailed Lemurs	Platypuses
Anteaters	Kangaroos	Rhinos	Jaguars	Wombats	Capybaras	Gorillas
Cats	Skunks	Butterflies	Dingoes	Snow Leopards	African Wild Dogs	Penguins
Whale Sharks	Wolverines	Warthogs	Caracals	Badgers	Seals	Hummingbirds
Pikas	Humpback Whales	Pumas	Lemonade	Llamas	Tulips	Ostriches
Sunflowers	Fennec Foxes	Sea Lions	Squirrels	Roses	Porcupines	Ice Cream

All titles by Victoria Blakemore

www.ingramcontent.com/pod-product-compliance
Lightning Source LLC
Chambersburg PA
CBHW051250020426
42333CB00025B/3144